THE 25 SALES HABITS

of HIGHLY SUCCESSFUL SALESPEOPLE

3RD EDITION

STEPHAN SCHIFFMAN

AMERICA'S #1 CORPORATE SALES TRAINER

Adams Media

New York   London   Toronto   Sydney   New Delhi

To your future

• • •

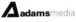

Adams Media
An Imprint of Simon & Schuster, Inc.
57 Littlefield Street
Avon, Massachusetts 02322

For information about special discounts for bulk purchases, please contact Simon
& Schuster Special Sales at 1-866-506-1949 or business@simonandschuster.com.

The Simon & Schuster Speakers Bureau can bring authors to your live event. For
more information or to book an event contact the Simon & Schuster Speakers
Bureau at 1-866-248-3049 or visit our website at www.simonspeakers.com.

Manufactured in the United States of America

30 29 28 27 26 25 24 23

Library of Congress Cataloging-in-Publication Data has been applied for.

ISBN 978-1-59869-757-5

Contents

Bonus Habits

Acknowledgments

I would like to thank the following people for their help with this book: my editor, Curt Schleier; my agent, Stephanie Kip Rosten; Laura Daly and Peter Archer at Adams Media; Monika Verma; and of course, Anne, Daniele, and Jennifer for their unceasing support.

Introduction to the Third Edition

For better or worse, we're all creatures of habit. We usually go to sleep and get up at the same time every day. Some people lay out their clothing the night before, some brush their hair the same number of times before they go to sleep.

I'm not a psychologist, but I suspect this kind of ritualistic behavior is a good thing. We have enough to worry about in our lives. So the chance to perform simple, day-to-day tasks without really thinking about them is a big plus. My guess is that if we had to reflect on every simple task we now do automatically—when we put out our clothes, how many times we brush our hair—we'd become paralyzed.

It's long been my contention that the best salespeople are also creatures of habit. You ask, "How can that be, Steve? You keep telling us we have to be flexible in our approach, be able to adjust to change." And that's certainly true.

The great salespeople are flexible enough to adopt new sales tools as they become available—from PowerPoint to text messaging. They know that they can't be locked into a single sales pitch, and they have to adjust what they say to each customer. They know the importance of the sales process—and their goals are always to get to the next step.

But that doesn't mean routine isn't important. The most important sales skill is prospecting. Those of you who've taken my courses or read my other books know that when I talk about prospecting, I mean finding someone new to speak to every single day.

Some people tell me they're able to rely exclusively on business from existing accounts. I'm never certain whether they mean they don't need to prospect because they have a rich vein they can continue to mine in companies with which they already do business . . . or that they're just order takers.

If they can really do that and are happy with the results, more power to them. But good salespeople—by my definition—can't afford not to prospect. They're never satisfied. They're hungry. They know they'll need good paydays four, five, six, seven months down the road, and that can only come from (depending on your sales cycle) clients they pick up today. (More on that in Habit #8.)

From the time I first got into sales, I made it my business to call fifteen leads every day; I've been in business for myself now almost three decades—and I still do that. It became a habit with me.

While many colleagues went straight to the coffee machine when they came into the office in the morning or to the watercooler to talk about last night's big game, I went directly to the phone.

At first, it took conscious effort to get on the phone. But that's not so true anymore. It's ingrained in me. And it can become ingrained in you. All you have to do is practice. Every morning when you get out of the car in the parking lot, step off the bus or ferry, or come up from the subway, set your priorities. And make making fifteen prospect calls every day priority number one.

Sure, it's difficult, but if I may borrow a marketing slogan from Nike, my advice to you is to just do it! Don't make twelve or ten calls. Don't call five people you've already spoken to and count them in your daily total. The process of ingraining good habits in your workday requires good and regular practice. It doesn't happen overnight. But what it boils down to is that (for me) building good habits is like building a stairway to success—and not just in sales.

Hall of Famer Cal Ripken, Jr., says his father used to tell him, practice doesn't make perfect. *Perfect* practice makes perfect. Cal Jr. said, "I used to think that was ridiculous. How are you gonna have fun if you're not going to fool around a little bit? But he felt if you want to build good habits, it's a lot better to take twenty-five to fifty ground balls the right way than to take 500 ground balls and screw around. My dad's message was all about building good habits, so when the game starts you can fall back on those habits and they seem natural."

And it wasn't just a matter of practicing fielding grounders. He got into the habit of watching the catcher and would move his position on the field based on the pitch, the count, the tendencies of the hitter, and even the tendencies of a manager. So if he knew a skipper liked to play hit and run in certain situations, he might shade over closer to second base.

For this new edition, I've added five new habits to help build your career. But no matter how many habits I suggest, they're all meaningless unless you ingrain them as part of your process, repeat them over and over again.

Cal Sr. is right: Perfect practice makes perfect.

Introduction

How has the sales landscape changed over the past ten or fifteen years?

That question occurred to me while I was working with a sales manager at a *Fortune* 500 firm who complained that his salespeople "still thought it was the early nineties."

The more I thought about his (accurate) observation, the more I was reminded that these habits, first outlined in book form years ago, really do highlight the strategies used nowadays by successful salespeople—the ones who have adapted to all the changes in today's competitive selling environment. And since then, my work with salespeople has convinced me of the point. This new edition reflects an opportunity for you to benefit from these habits for success by incorporating them into your sales routine. (And, yes, you can add a good habit to your routine—just as you can add a bad one!)

• • •

For my money, selling is the most exciting job in the world. With the right organization, it gives you unlimited income potential, freedom, and a clear means to take control of your career and your life. I believe it beats any other occupation hands down. But there's a problem.

In the seminars that my company conducts, the first question we ask of salespeople is, "What's the one thing you would like to change about your job?" The answer we get is always the same: "The attitude people have toward what we do for a living!"

Large segments of the public simply don't trust salespeople. Part of that has to do with personal contact with flimflam artists. Part of it has to do with media images of salespeople. Whether it's a crazy used-car salesman in an obnoxious commercial or a shifty, fast-talking wheeler-dealer on some crime drama, salespeople *never* seem to come off in the media as hardworking, concerned, accountable professionals. The negative stereotypes are reinforced thousands of times a day.

Of course, there really are people out there who look for a quick buck, shout a lot, and keep an eye open for new office space when customers have problems. But this book won't help them. This book is for us. The good guys. The salespeople who want to build business relationships, deliver results, and stand behind what's delivered. But when we knock on the door, who does our prospect think of? Those thousand yellow-jacketed pitchmen who talk too fast and don't care in the least about the prospect's viewpoint, that's who! Sometimes we lose sales—not because of what we've done, but because of what the people who have come before us have done.

This book will help you demonstrate the poise, professionalism, and accountability that is *required* of today's successful salesperson. This book will show you twenty-five traits that will help you instantly distinguish yourself from the amateurs your prospect may be confusing you with. This book is your blueprint for achievement in the fastest-paced, most dynamic profession in business.

• • •

Earlier, I pointed out that a lot has changed in business—and in sales—over the last decade. Before we move on to the habits for success, let's review three of the most important points today's salesperson must bear in mind.

First and most important, you must remember that your prospects are more value-conscious and *information-conscious* than ever. From the first instant of your contact with a new sales prospect, you must be prepared to demonstrate your patterns of success with previous customers, and you had better be able to discuss, chapter and verse, the specific benefits you've delivered. Similarly, you must also bring to your first meeting with the prospect a recognizable expertise in your business area. That doesn't mean you need to memorize the encyclopedia before you close a sale, and it certainly doesn't mean that you should throw around a lot of fancy language the prospect won't understand. But in this time-pressed, data-sensitive age of ours, you must demonstrate to the prospect that your organization brings a unique and impressive knowledge and skill base to its business relationships.

Secondly (and this comes as a surprise to many salespeople), you must take an aggressive presentation stance that does *not* necessarily focus on the prospect's own perceived "needs." For decades, we were told to focus exclusively on these self-defined "needs" of the prospect, but a more accurate way to state the matter now would be to say that you are responsible for helping to define the requirements. With staffs stretched to the breaking point and managers juggling fifteen different balls at once, your prospect may not even *know* about an impending problem or lost opportunity! These days, when you "need" something, it's usually because the president of your company has told you to attend to a particular problem—and believe me, in those circumstances, you don't wait around for a salesperson to give you a call. You head out to the widget factory and set it up yourself. So don't focus so much on "needs." The key to selling in today's fast-paced environment is to ask people what they do, how they do it, when and where they do it, why they do it that way, and how you can help them do it better. The successful salesperson today is more attuned to the "do" than to the "need."

Finally, today's successful salesperson is willing to think ahead. That means consistently looking for the next step in the sales process. That means prospecting for tomorrow—and maintaining a prospect base, even if you're given an existing account base to work with. That means anticipating common objections and avoiding unproductive exchanges with prospects. And that means being willing to change approaches that aren't working now, even if they worked in the past. In the final analysis, thinking ahead means taking responsibility for your own career. For the real salesperson, the person who loves a challenge and loves to be in the driver's seat, that's no problem at all.

• • •

Make no mistake. You're going to have to fight to win and keep customers. Intense competition is a fact of life in today's market. The time for complacency in sales, if there ever was one, is long past.

There are a lot of salespeople out there today competing for the business you work hard to obtain. Some of them do a very good job, make a lot of money, and stick around, building satisfying careers that last for decades. Others try to wing it and burn out. I've worked with both kinds. The habits that distinguish the former from the latter are in this book. They can work for you.

Good luck!
—*Stephan Schiffman*
New York, New York

If It Doesn't Work, Fix It

In the introduction to this edition, I mentioned the importance of working at something until it becomes ingrained in you. I used the example of getting into the habit of making the same number of prospect calls the first thing every morning, no matter what. Clearly, that's a good habit to get into, and over the next hundred or so pages, I'm going to give you more to try.

I'm not unmindful of the possibility that you already have a lot of business habits, personal techniques you developed over the years in the way you make calls, prepare presentations, and even make the presentations themselves. But not all habits are good.

The reality is that if you're reading this book, there's a good chance that something's bothering you, either consciously or subconsciously, about your sales process.

Knowing or sensing that something is wrong is easy. Figuring out what it is, though, can be (and usually is) difficult. And that's not just true for salespeople.

A writer friend of mine regularly regales me with stories about the hours he's spent working on an article—or

1

more accurately, not working on one. He'll sit in front of his computer and just stare. Why? He knows something is wrong with the piece; he just doesn't know what it is.

So after a while of doing little, if anything, he leaves his word-processing program and starts to play Free Cell. (For you Mac fanatics, that's a game that comes with Microsoft Windows.) He jokes that he doesn't play *a* game; no, he plays a Free Cell *tournament*. Then he returns to his work and reads it over from the beginning. In the process, he corrects grammatical mistakes and typos and tries to ascertain what's bothering him, what's wrong with his story.

If he's still stumped, he goes back to playing games— but this time it's a solitaire tournament. "I like to think I'm ambi-game-derous," he jokes.

Eventually, of course, he figures out what's wrong, corrects it, and is then able to complete his story. My point is if you think something is wrong in your sales process, there probably is something wrong. I'm a great believer in instinct. But it is important that you stop and review your process to see if you can figure out what it is that's out of whack. And then fix it. Chances are, it's something simple.

For example, I needed a special product and called a sales rep I knew in London. He wasn't there, but he returned my call. Only this time I was out; he left his name and the hours he'd be in the office. But he didn't leave his phone number. What's the point of that?

I was away from the office and didn't have his number with me, so I couldn't call him. When I got back from my trip a week later, we played telephone tag for about ten days until I gave up and placed an order elsewhere.

Another sales rep I know has been leaving the same basic message when making cold calls for twenty years—pretty much unsuccessfully. I'm sure both men are surprised when prospects don't return their calls—though one has been using the same approach for two decades with little to show for it and the other always assuming that a potential customer has his telephone number.

To go to another extreme, I know that there are salespeople who never leave a message. That way they can pester the individual forever, expecting eventually to get them on the phone. What's the logic of calling someone twenty or twenty-five times hoping to get them on the phone?

If you're not doing well, if people aren't returning your calls, if you're not getting appointments, if you're not closing sales, well, then you know something is wrong. You have to re-examine how you approach the sales process, figure out what's wrong, and change it. Go step by step; examine your cold-call ratios, the questions you ask on a first appointment, the way you prepare presentations.

However, the problem isn't always clear-cut. All the people I've mentioned here, for example, are decent salespeople. They make okay money, in large measure because other parts of their game work well. If you're getting by, it's easy to overlook the fact that something is holding you back from being a great salesperson and making big money.

So I want to go back to my writer friend. Every time he returns to his computer from a break—even if everything is going well—*he rereads the story he's working on from the beginning*. Every time he does that, he finds improvements he can make.

Can you do any less for yourself? I sit down after every presentation—whether I clinch a sale or not—and review what I did step by step to see what I did wrong and to see what I could do better. Of course, I usually give myself high marks on those presentations that lead to a signed contract. But even then, I find I've made a misstep somewhere along the line.

And when I don't clinch a sale, there are mistakes galore. Mistakes, by themselves, don't bother me. (See Bonus Habit #1.) But what I look for is patterns of bad behavior. And that's what I look to correct and fine-tune.

Once a month I examine all my activity for the previous four weeks. How are my cold-call ratios? Am I getting through to enough people? Am I getting a sufficient number of appointments from the leads I speak to? Are these appointments leading to presentations?

Self-examination is not easy. Sometimes you need to bring in a manager to help you see the forest for the trees. But it is imperative. I see more and more experienced salespeople come to my classes who've allowed themselves to become comfortable with their bad habits. I always ask them what they would do differently. Invariably, they scratch their heads and can't come up with an answer.

If you're scratching your head and can't come up with an answer to what you would do to improve yourself, you're not going to change. And you're certainly not going to get better.

Communicate the Message that It Is Sound Business to Trust You

I've trained over a half-million salespeople. And the more salespeople I run into, the more exposure I get to various "tricks of the trade"—little corners salespeople cut in order to get ahead (or so they think) over the short term. The only problem is, too many of these "tricks of the trade" undercut an essential objective: that of constantly sending and reinforcing the message that it is a good business decision to trust you.

The "raffle" and its consequences when it comes to building long-term partnerships

I know a car dealer who uses a trick to get people to come into his showroom. He opens up the white pages, finds a name, calls the person, and says, "Hi, Mr. Jones, this is Mike Johnson at Johnson Used Cars. You've just won our raffle! Come on in and collect a turkey!" What he never says is that he really wants the person to come in and collect two turkeys: one to put in the oven, and the other for the driveway. (By the way, there is no raffle; the turkeys are bought as premiums for anyone who walks through the door.)

The same salesperson would call up someone at random and claim to have found his wallet, "just to get his attention," then launch into his pitch. How much would you trust an approach like that?

I'm not trying to be harsh toward those who sell automobiles for a living. Some of the most effective salespeople I know sell used cars. But I am trying to say something about *this* used-car salesman. By starting off with "Hey, you've won a free turkey," he is using a cheap trick. It seems to me that it was no coincidence that he sells cars to match. Word gets around about that sort of thing.

If you sell turkeys, talk about turkeys. If you sell cars, talk about cars. Talk about exactly why it makes perfect sense to buy the one you have to offer. Beware of the tricks of the trade. If they come at the expense of your credibility, they're too expensive.

"Follow me!"

The successful salesperson makes a good leader because he or she inspires trust. I think that the truly successful salespeople today—and, by the way, this is what I see in world-class sales forces—have the personal magnetism and the self-assurance to say to people, "Follow me," and thereby win long-term, happy customers. That kind of authority only comes with complete, unflinching confidence that you can deliver results for your prospect. If you're right, your customers trust you—and follow you.

Building trustworthiness, then, means *building leadership skills*. That's not to say you should practice railroading your customers! All the confidence and authority in the world won't change the I-found-that-wallet-you-never-really-lost scam into a way to build trust. It means understanding your product or service, understanding what your prospects do for a living, and assuming responsibility for delivering results to your customers, no matter what. Prospects can sense when this is what you're offering, and they like it.

What makes a good leader?

- A good leader has a vision.
- A good leader commands respect.
- A good leader sees the big picture.
- A good leader knows when to change direction.
- A good leader points out problem areas and is ready to discuss solutions.
- A good leader has confidence in both approach and attitude.
- And a good leader is accountable.

All of these traits add up to true trustworthiness.

The real thing

Too many salespeople focus on whether or not they have learned to appear trustworthy. That's not the point! You want to develop an earned reputation for following through on everything—and I mean every syllable—that comes out of your mouth. That means, for one thing, absolute punctuality. If you say you'll call at 9:00 a.m., then call at 9:00 a.m., and not 9:02 a.m. Better yet, call at 8:55 a.m. and be willing to be put on hold! Some salespeople take this principle and turn it into a recipe for annoyance; others display the spark of professionalism necessary to demonstrate dependability and consistency as personal hallmarks.

If you think such "minor details" don't have any real persuasive power, I have to disagree with you. At the beginning of your relationship with a prospect, those details are all he or she has to go on. They're the only tool you have! Spout lavish promises, and fail to follow through on the details, and you'll be like every other salesperson. But say you're ready, within the next five minutes, to fax or e-mail over a quote that completely meets all the prospect's specifications, then *do it* . . . and you're one in a million

Relationships are built on trust, and trust is built on evidence of all kinds. This does not mean that you must show that you're subservient—that's the opposite of being a leader! You must demonstrate that you are unfailingly dependable in all things, big and small, and you must make a habit of delivering what you promised (or, preferably, more). Then you will be in a position to say with authority, "Follow me."

HABIT #3

Ask the Right Questions

Ask important questions. Ask real questions. If you need to rely on "How's the weather?" or "Have a nice weekend?" for your opening, fine. But thereafter, base everything you ask on a simple principle: Never waste the prospect's time. That may seem like an obvious point, but it certainly isn't treated like one by most salespeople! Know when it's time to move beyond the litany of pointless observations on décor, golf, the weather, or whatever. You came here on a business appointment. There will come a point at which your client will be ready to move past the small talk. Do so, tactfully.

A single question to help you make the transition into the "business end" of the conversation
How do you start asking the important questions? I'm going to suggest that you start with a simple one—a question that may seem to have nothing to do with your visit, but that will actually yield some remarkable insights into the kind of person you're working with.

"Just out of curiosity, Ms. Allen—how did you get this job?"

That will ease you into the "business end" of the visit quite nicely, and will also encourage your contact to open up to you. After your prospect has had the chance to answer in whatever degree of detail he or she feels comfortable with, you might continue by saying what you have in mind—why you're talking to the person in the first place—and explaining why you're going over this (so your later questions will make more sense).

> "Ms. Allen, we handle the top-selling line of widgets in the United States of America. Let me tell you a little bit about how we work. My only job during this first meeting is to find out about your business; I didn't come here to sell anything today. I mention that because I wanted to ask you a few questions about your store, to find out if I really can help you boost your sales volume. Have you got a moment for that?"

What do you do once you've told the prospect a (very) little about your business solutions?

Assuming you get a "yes" to the question that ends that little speech (and that's a pretty good bet), you can then move on to the big questions.

Question One—The Past: "Have you ever used any of our widgets before?" ("If so, how did they work out?")

Question Two—The Present: "Just out of curiosity, what widget are you presently using?" ("How do you feel about it?")

Question Three—The Future: "Tell me something; what do the next six months look like for you in terms of widget use?" ("How do you plan to use widgets to reach goal X?")

If you feel uncomfortable moving into "serious" areas, like whether or not the firm uses or might use your products, but you still feel certain that you have passed the point at which you can discuss last night's baseball game, there are a number of middle-ground questions you can pose before getting to the heart of the matter. Here are some suggestions:

- "Tell me, what kind of customers do you serve?"
- "What other locations do you have?" (Or, "Where are your headquarters located?")
- "What kind of sales force do you use?"
- "How long has the firm been in business?"
- "What kinds of challenges do you face in this business/industry?"

Such questions may well yield important information for you, and can serve as an effective "bridge" to the main point of your visit. But beware of overreliance on such middle-ground questions; my guess is that your contact is, like most of us these days, short on time. Most prospects will appreciate your getting to the point in short order, and you can do this without jeopardizing the emerging relationship.

The last "right question"

The last "right question" of your first visit usually sounds something like this:

> "You know, Mr. Jones, I've learned a lot today, and I want to thank you for taking the opportunity to talk to me. Let me tell you what I usually do at this stage. I think we're at that point now where I need to set up another appointment for us, one where I can come back after having sorted through everything I've learned here, and show you what we may be able to do for your company. Is Tuesday at three okay?"

Habit #4

Take the Lead

Tell the prospect where you are at any given point in the sales cycle. Don't be afraid to steer the conversation in the direction you want it to go.

Here's what it might sound like

"Mr. Prospect, I want to thank you very much for taking time out to see me today. I know we have a lot to go over, but during this part of the visit what I usually do is give some information about my company and what we do. We've been in business since . . . ."

"Mr. Prospect, at this stage I'd like to ask a couple of simple questions that will help me find out ways we can help you."

"Well, now that we've come this far, Mr. Prospect, I'll tell you what I'd like to do. I'd like to take these notes and go back to my office and see if we can work up a proposal for you, then meet again next week. Would Friday at two be okay?"

"Certainly good to meet with you again, Mr. Prospect. Now that we've worked up this proposal, I think it would be a good idea for me to take a few minutes to just summarize it for you here, and then answer any questions you may have."

"So that's our proposal, Mr. Prospect. I have a feeling we will really be able to put this program into place for you successfully. At this point in the process, my feeling is that the sooner we get this underway, the better it will be for your company. Is Saturday the twelfth of December a good day to start?"

The perils of doing anything and everything to avoid offending the prospect

How many presentations are sabotaged by salespeople who want to avoid "offending"—and never get around to mentioning the reason they stepped in the door in the first place? Take charge. Make a conscious choice to inform the prospect about where you both are in the process. The alternative is long, "good" meetings that end in that odd, result-free limbo that leaves neither party sure what to do next.

We don't live in a perfect world. We live in a world of complex people who have complex thinking patterns—people whose next action may not be obvious to us. It follows, then, that we run the risk of having the prospect stop us and say, "Hold on—wait a minute. I'm not ready for that yet. You're moving too fast for me."

So what?

You need that information. You need to know where there is still a problem to be worked on. If you don't know where there's a problem, you won't be able to close the sale. And it's far better to isolate a problem through a consistent system of "sequence updates" (as I like to call them) than to wait until the last minute, ask for the business, and then find out there was something important you should have been paying attention to but weren't.

Getting the information you'll need to move ahead in the sales cycle—even if it's not what you want to hear

Sometimes, as a result of these updates and the feedback you receive from them, you will isolate issues the prospect has not yet brought to the surface. You may find that, even though you went in the door thinking about selling Widget A, and even though the prospect seems interested enough in Widget A, the questions that keep coming up as you try to move the process along seem to concern the applications you know can only be obtained through Widget B! Your objective is to solve problems—not to make the prospect fit your preconceptions. So you move on to Widget B. But you can only do this because you've listened to the feedback your updates have yielded.

Let's be clear on one thing: Sales cycles will vary from industry to industry and from customer to customer. What that means in plain English is that you never know when someone's going to agree to buy something. I'm not suggesting that you try to manhandle the prospect. Even if you issue the updates I'm talking about, you still have to be willing to work with the prospect, every step of the way. The key point is you can't do that unless you both know where you are—and where you're going.

HABIT #5

Listen, Learn, and Lead

In the previous chapter, I discussed how important it is to lead your customer to where you (ideally) both want to go. But that begs the question, why would anyone want to follow you?

The reason is simple. It's because you are a leader. The best salespeople are—and that obviously means more than being the person with the highest sales for the month or the year. That's a superficial way to measure leadership—especially sales leadership.

A number of things factor into sales leadership. One of the most important is product knowledge. You know your product or service better than anyone else on the planet. You know how to adapt your products to fill a variety of your customers' needs. You know your pricing structure. You can make a deal that the customer can afford and still allows you a good profit.

And, most important of all, you demonstrate your willingness to walk the extra mile. I think it was Groucho

Marx who said the key to success was honesty and fair dealing. "Once you can fake that, you've got it made."

I don't subscribe to that notion. There's really too much at stake here, including your livelihood. And, quite frankly, if you can't genuinely be honest, if you don't really care about your customers, then perhaps you should consider another line of work.

Caring, trying to do what's best for everyone involved, is an important leadership tool, one that will get a prospect to follow all the way to a signed contract. The key is to get as much information as you can.

The Power of Twelve

Therein lies what I call the Power of Twelve. As noted earlier, one of your leadership skills is knowledge. No one knows your product lines as well as you do. Now your goal is to reach that same level of knowledge about your customer. In order to fully understand the prospect's company and its needs, you need to see as many as twelve people in the organization.

Spending time with a buyer is just not enough. Ideally, you want to go to the manufacturing plant to see the way the people on the line make their products—hopefully discovering ways yours is superior to what is currently in use.

Spend time with the marketing staff to see how and to whom they sell their products. Speak to the company's sales force, its executives. And at every stop, ask all the people you meet how and why they do what they do and whether there's a way your product can help them do it better.

By the time you're through, you should know more about the company than its CEO. To do that, you have to listen to what they say. Every person you meet may be the one that can provide you entrée to this account, that special nugget of information that turns the tide in your favor. The key is listening to as many people as you can to truly learn about a prospect's business. When someone believes you are genuinely interested in what they have to say, they're more likely to open up and tell you more about the business.

One of my favorite stories is about a rep who had one major account. When I asked him how many people were involved in making decisions on purchasing the nearly 400 products he sold there, he told me 200. When I asked him how many he called on regularly, he told me four.

How could he possibly sell to any depth if he only listened to and learned from four of 200 people? When I reviewed his efforts, it soon became clear to me that all he received were superficial orders. There was a lot of money (and commission) left on the table because he didn't follow this basic principle of the Power of Twelve. So he couldn't listen, he couldn't learn, *and* he couldn't lead.

What could he have done? He had entrée at this company. He could have walked around and introduced himself. Likely, he'd have become aware of other projects the company was working on, which would have put him in a position of suggesting more of his products.

If I am starting to sound repetitive and boring, it is because when I realize I have something that works, I'm going to do it over and over again. I will make it a habit. It's like a golf swing. If you're getting to the green from the tee, why would you change?

One of the basic axioms I teach is that the more complex the sale, the more you need to get the prospect involved. And the best way to do that is to listen, learn, and lead.

Engage the Prospect

Engaging the prospect is a subtle undertaking; it is difficult to define. In fact, it's easier for me to tell you what it's not. Engaging the prospect is not reacting instantaneously, as if by reflex, to every comment or perceived disapproval. Consider this exchange.

> Prospect: The last time we worked in this area, I'll never forget, the first session was on a Monday morning, and . . .

> You: Oh, well, we can work on Mondays. Mondays are no problem.

> Prospect: Well, actually, what I was going to say was that since it was a Monday morning, we didn't have quite the eager spirit that we might have preferred . . .

You: I see, I see. Well, we can do it on any day you want.

That's not engaging anyone. That's ping-pong. Engaging your prospect means going beyond slap-shot, automatic exchanges. It requires that you respond so clearly to stated or unstated requirements (not all of which will have to do with your product or service) that you establish a core of understanding and a framework within which both you and your prospect can solve important problems. You will have to find, for yourself, the best way to establish that connection, given the particular dynamics of a given prospect's age, position, gender, even race, in comparison with yours. It is pointless to ignore such differences among people, and virtually suicidal not to accommodate them in a sales setting.

Your prospect's unique circumstances

Every prospect is different. Every prospect reacts differently to what you have to say. Some seem to have all the time in the world; others consider a fifteen-minute meeting to be a major crisis in time management. Some have made careers out of being skeptical; others pride themselves on freethinking, even outrageous approaches to problems. The point is that you cannot earn the respect of all of them with a single "script" designed to "handle the first few minutes." You must identify what is important to any given prospect, and then learn how to appeal to those values.

Here are some general suggestions on drawing out your prospect and initiating meaningful initial conversations. Of course, you will have to adapt them to fit particular situations.

Discuss that with which you are comfortable and familiar. Avoid venturing opinions on abstract expressionism if you know nothing about that school of modern art; do offer your insights on model trains, Disney collectibles, or memory improvements if the topic in question is one you have an informed interest in. Your confidence in the subject you select—and connect somehow to your prospect—will carry over. (Note: There is an advantage to beginning an exchange by focusing on your own observations and experiences—adroitly and tactfully, of course. Doing so takes some of the pressure off your prospect, who will be expecting you to try to "draw him in.")

Discuss the surroundings. The office you will be sitting in is a reflection of its occupant. Surely you can find, with little difficulty, something that will serve as a positive conversational starting point that has to do with the way your prospect has chosen to decorate his or her surroundings.

Support the prospect in subtle ways

When the person starts to talk about himself, "lean in" to the conversation. I also put down the pen I'm using to take notes. This serves as a subtle validation that the prospect's experiences are inherently interesting. (It is almost always good to get the prospect discussing his or her own experiences. People who talk about themselves are more relaxed than people who don't.)

Show care by really caring. Remember, you're there to help. When the prospect outlines a problem, show the same concern you would if it were yours. (After all, you want it to be yours!)

HABIT #7

Find Key Requirements

Should you set your goal as that of "finding customers who need the product"? All the time? The answer is more complicated than you might think.

News flash: the economy has changed—and you should, too, if you want to succeed

Most of us who are selling today are not creating a new market. That is to say, we're not following the time-honored advice to "find a need and fill it," because, on the whole, we can't. Our economy has been eradicating basic needs on a historically unprecedented scale for almost a half-century now, and it's done a pretty darned good job. Not a perfect job, of course, but a good enough job to change the way most salespeople must operate. What today's salespeople must do to succeed is find requirements they can fill among those sought-after, qualified buyers who know full well that the choice is theirs when it comes to choosing the new widget service.

We have a lot of automobiles in this country. We have a lot of copiers. And we have a whole bunch of health-care plans available, too. If it is your job to sell an automobile, a copier, or a health-care plan, you will have to come up with something new and exciting about your particular offer for a given buyer who, these days, can be counted on more and more to have some experience with your product or service category. You will have to tailor your approach to the requirements you are identifying within such prospect groups. Otherwise, you will have some problems.

Find the prospect who fits your profile of a happy customer, and work from there

This is not to say that there is no such thing as a first-time car buyer, or a company that is shopping around for its first health plan. Obviously, the patterns of "new" buyers will vary from region to region and from industry to industry. My point is, most good salespeople I meet do not make "virgin" prospects their core concern. Their objective, typically, is not to identify a need for the widget but to get a lead on the type of widget buyer/user whose requirements they can satisfy better than anyone else—then make some striking comparisons to that person.

Find your segment, your area of expertise, your niche. Learn to classify common concerns and problems shared by the types of "educated" customers you know you have been able to satisfy. Then prospect for that person. Of course, you aren't going to turn anyone down who doesn't fit your profile but still wants to buy from you. But most successful salespeople I know develop a sense of who the likely customer is—and then put themselves in front of as many of those types of people as possible.

With someone who's been using Brand X widgets for twenty years, your goal isn't to identify the need—it is to unearth the requirements that will get your prospect to consider changing to your Brand Y widgets.

Does he require a better service plan? More flexibility with payments? A better price? Frequent contact with you the salesperson? There are a million variables. Often the requirements will be difficult to gauge; perhaps the prospect himself has not fully identified them. That's where you come in.

The salesperson as tactful educator and facilitator—not steamroller

Of course, there are some fields of sales in which the primary focus may well be on first-time buyers; insurance comes to mind. Here, too, however, it is a little simplistic to look at the process as simply "finding a need." Any good insurance agent can tell you that a major part of his job is education—filling in the knowledge gaps the first-time buyer brings to the table, and then providing the information necessary for that person to make the right choice. This requires no small degree of tact, patience, and persistence—all for a considerable period of time after the need is found.

Think about it. If you're a person who "needs" life insurance, and who does not require any assistance or new information to get to that point, what are you going to do? Call the life insurance company!

Remember: When dealing with a customer who already uses a competing product or service—as we so often must—we have to remember that the need itself has already been established. It has been so firmly established that the person has opted to take time out of a very busy schedule to meet with you and discuss it. More sales than you might imagine have been lost because of a salesperson's inability to grasp that the focus with the "educated" customer must be on how to identify and meet new requirements that the current product or service is not meeting.

The importance of perspective—and patience—in dealing with your prospects

Keep things in perspective here. No one is suggesting you should not talk up your products—and vigorously! It's all a question of how. Prattling on about how wonderful Brand Y widgets are, when compared to no widgets, is suicidal. Discussing the specific ways Brand Y widgets will deliver more, perform better, or make for a more attractive budget than Brand X is the way you will make the sale.

Look at each lead as a sales relationship—and remember that relationships take time to develop.

HABIT #8

Know the Sales Timetable

Knowing, understanding, and using a timetable is one of the most important elements of the sales process—yet ironically, it is often overlooked and almost invariably left out of sales training. It is ignored with equal vigor by salespeople and sales managers alike.

I think that's true because the process seems more difficult to explain and understand than it really is. So let's start out with a real-world example.

You have an appointment tomorrow at 9 a.m. with an important prospect seventy miles away. It's a straight highway run that normally takes ninety minutes. But because you'll be traveling during rush hour, you allow an extra thirty minutes for the trip. So you want to leave your house at 7 a.m., and to do that you set your alarm for 6 a.m.

In a nutshell, that simple example also illustrates a sales timetable. Basically, you plan your sales efforts working backwards from your customer's needs. Here's an example.

Captain Andy, a major American cereal manufacturer I just made up, is planning a brand extension. The company's marketing and research staff has concluded that a new variety of breakfast food will capture that all-important three-year-old demographic. So in a year's time, supermarkets around the country will be flooded with Captain Andy cereals, choice nuggets of chocolate, fresh fruits, and sugar.

That's twelve months off, but if you're in the packaging business, and you want to sell the company boxes for the new product, obviously you can't wait until the product is about to hit the shelves before you go in and make a pitch for your boxes. You should be calling the prospect now, before any firm packaging decisions have been made. If you wait six months—or even as little as three months—you'll just be wasting your time.

If you miss the critical cycle, you'll be locked out on two levels—developing and delivering the initial packaging for the product release, and then continuous delivery as the presumably successful product captures market share.

This is true for many if not most commercial products. If you sell copiers, you have to be aware of when a prospect's current leases are up. If it's insurance, you have to know when a company's policies come up for renewal.

But—and this is critical—you not only have to know your customer's buying cycle, you have to know your sell cycle, as well. Let's use that first example. You design, create, and manufacture packaging for a variety of industries.

You've heard that Captain Andy is looking to develop a new cereal it wants to market in twelve months. Typically your own sales cycle is six weeks—that is, on average, it takes a month and a half from the time you first contact a company until you get a signed contract. Then it usually takes three to four weeks before your design team comes up with a package a customer approves. And then it can take another three weeks to buy cardboard and ink, find time on your presses, and get those boxes shipped to the cereal manufacturer's plants.

These are made-up numbers of course, but as you can see it takes at least about three months from the first contact to product delivery. So you have to work backwards, from the company's buy cycle to your sell cycle to decide when to start a significant push—or when it's too late.

In the case of Captain Andy, you would have to be in selling at least three months before the company expects to start the cereal lines moving in its plants.

Knowing your timetable is important in a couple of other key areas, as well. For one thing, the timetable is a way to gauge how well you are doing. Let's say you work in an industry where your sales cycle is six months. Then it takes another six weeks for bills to be paid and another six weeks for you to collect your commission check. That means by March, you should know how you've done for the year.

Also, the cycle is, or at least can serve as, an incentive. If you understand the timetable, you recognize the importance of prospecting every day. If you don't prospect today, there'll be no commission check nine months down the road. And if that doesn't get you on the phone, nothing will.

Convert the Leads that "Fall into Your Lap"

It's a dream come true.

You're on the job, minding your own business, when suddenly someone calls, seemingly out of the blue, and virtually asks you for your business. Wow!

I know what the first temptation is. You want to close the sale. Life is tough enough; you spend all day building, establishing, persuading. Now along comes The Sale You Deserve, and you're sure as heck not going to let it slip through your fingers. So you start to move in.

Don't.

It will take some discipline. (Let's be honest; it will take a lot of discipline.) But if you really want to move the lead from the other end of the receiver onto your commission check, I promise you that the surest way to do it is to take a deep breath, count to three, and follow a few simple steps.

Three steps to follow:

1. *Back off and establish some kind of relationship.* If this really is someone you've never spoken to before, you don't know whether or not a brusque, let's-get-right-down-to-business, well-of-course-we-can-solve-your-problem approach is going to work. It may backfire spectacularly—and often does. So exchange a few pleasantries and get a feeling for the kind of person you're talking to.

2. *Find out what's going on.* Say, "I'm really glad you got in touch with me. Listen, do you mind if I ask what prompted your call?" This is very important! No sale exists in a vacuum, and you have to know exactly what you're dealing with. Things may not be what they seem! Sometimes people call and sound like they're going to sign on, but really they need generous amounts of tender loving care. Establish your surroundings; get the information. Don't succumb to the temptation to sell—it may be too early.

3. *Ask to set up an in-person appointment.* Yes, even if the person tries to close the sale himself on the phone. (Unless, of course, you're involved with telemarketing.) You need to establish a personal bond.

Don't assume you've got a sure thing. Sales is a numbers game. Your objective is to turn the odds in your favor in as many different ways, and on as many different occasions, as humanly possible.

If you do that over the long haul, it will pay off handsomely.

Know How to Make Your Product or Service Fit Somewhere Else

How can you adapt an existing product or service to satisfy a prospect?

In my seminars, I talk a lot about a product or service in terms of its malleability (a word that means "flexibility" or "capacity for being adapted").

Dentists use gold and silver for fillings because of the malleability of those metals, which are easily manipulated and provide a complete, secure fit over and within a cavity. Along the same lines, you might want to think about the ways your product or service can be adjusted or customized for new prospects to meet specific requirements.

The paper clip

Let's take a look at a simple example. Suppose you're in the paper-clip business. How many ways do you think you could use paper clips? Obviously, you can think of a paper clip as a small metal item used to fasten sheets of paper together. But if you stop and think about it for a moment, you'll realize that people use paper clips for all kinds of different purposes. Some people twist them into makeshift cotter pins; some people use them to clean out hard-to-reach places on office equipment; some people use them to fix eyeglasses; some people make decorative chains out of them. Years ago, I even used (with great care!) two paper clips as a tiny clamp to extract a stubborn disk that would not eject from my computer's drive.

Beyond holding sheets of paper together, there are probably hundreds of different uses for a paper clip. Are there hundreds of different uses for your product or service that you may not have considered before? Before you dismiss this possibility, keep in mind that you don't need to think up hundreds of new ideas to boost your sales. You just need to think of one.

Baking soda is for cooking, right? Well, it can be . . . but for some strange reason the Arm & Hammer people insist on running these ads promoting its use as a refrigerator deodorizer. (By the way, do you know anyone who uses baking soda that way these days?)

We all know you're not supposed to play with your food. Or are you? The people who make Jell-O think you should. They launched a huge media campaign that was intended solely to familiarize consumers with the idea of making Jiggler cookie cutter shapes out of gelatin, then letting the kids play with the Jell-O before devouring it. They gave away the Jiggler molds with any Jell-O purchase. An informal study of the market results (that is, me watching what the people in front of me in line have brought to the checkout counter) yields the admittedly unscientific observation that a heck of a lot more people than usual seem to be buying Jell-O—and buying it six, eight, or even twelve packs at a time.

That's product malleability.

Ask yourself!

Does what you sell work in only one way? Or can you adjust it? Can you make it serve some new purpose or function? Can you present it in a different light or to a different group of people? The key lies in opening your own mind to new possibilities, then following through.

This is not to say that you have to become another Henry Ford or Thomas Edison to make this principle work for you. Keep it simple to begin with. You can start with just one variation. If it's a winner, you may very well find that it can change not only your career in sales but perhaps also the business you work for!

Pretend You're a Consultant (Because You Are)

Treat all your sales work as a consulting assignment.

Many years ago, I found myself hopelessly stuck while working with a new prospect. I was trying to develop a program for him, and things simply weren't working out.

So here's what I did. I said, "Charlie, rather than go any further with this, let me think about what we've talked about here and come back next week with a couple of ideas. Then, if you like them, we can continue our discussion." He agreed to that; I eventually closed the sale.

It was shortly after that meeting that I realized what I had done. I had taken the same approach I would normally take with a client who was simply asking for an evaluation of the problems on his firm's sales staff. I had taken the "sell" sign down for a moment and come to grips with the fact that, since I did not yet have an adequate assessment of the prospect's problems, I could not offer him a solution.

There's a catch to selling from the mindset of the consultant. You have to be willing to stop and think once in a while.

Solving problems

The best salespeople are professional problem solvers. If you sell cars, then you should consider yourself in the business of solving transportation problems. If you sell copiers, then you should consider yourself in the business of solving photocopying problems. If you sell cell phones or PDAs, then you should consider yourself in the business of solving communications problems. But you have to know and understand the problem before you can try to solve it. You have to be willing to walk in the door without any preconceived notions about how best to unravel the problems identified.

For many salespeople, the consulting principle can be put on an even simpler footing. If you sell to other companies, you should consider yourself in the business of solving profitability problems. That's the key concern you will ultimately address: how to increase profitability. Everything you do, every proposal you offer, should lead eventually to the goal of increasing the level of your client's firm's profitability. Weigh your goals and your approaches against this standard, and you will have gone a long way toward achieving sales success.

If you're not interested in helping people solve problems, then I'm going to respectfully suggest that you're not in the right business. If you can't break everything you do down into something that helps another person reach an important goal, you will either base your sales on manipulating others or fail to persuade prospects that you offer anything of value. Either path leads inexorably to burnout and/or constant rejection. You definitely don't need that.

You could look it up

The dictionary defines *consult* as "to seek advice, information, or guidance from." To me, this definition encapsulates exactly the relationship between a qualified prospect and a professional salesperson. You as a salesperson are there to advise the prospect about ways you can help solve existing problems, to provide all necessary information relative to solving those problems, and to provide the necessary guidance that will result in a harmonious professional association.

Act like a consultant . . . because that's really what you are!

Ask for the Next Appointment While You're on the First Visit

This is perhaps the easiest piece of advice to follow in this book. Yet it is also a step that salespeople routinely ignore. Many are even afraid to take it even though they know it has worked wonders for others!

A young salesperson once actually said to me, "Steve, that's not my place. I'm in the prospect's office. He's showing me a courtesy by seeing me in the first place. If I'm going to go back there for a second visit, the prospect should ask me."

Baloney!

You initiated the contact in the first place. You have made it clear at every point in the process that your objective is to help the prospect. You have demonstrated that you are interested primarily in solving a problem for him. Why on earth shouldn't you ask the prospect for the next appointment so you can show how you would implement the solution?

Excuses, excuses

This point is—to me, at any rate—so basic that it requires little argument in its favor. Yet it never ceases to amaze me how much bewildered amazement greets me when I suggest it to salespeople. Here are some actual answers I've received from salespeople in response to the suggestion that they set up their next appointment during the first visit.

"I can't ask for the appointment; I don't know when I'll be back in the area."

"I can't ask for the appointment; I don't know how long it will take me to write the proposal."

"I can't ask for the appointment; I don't have a quote ready for the prospect yet."

"I can't ask for the appointment; he may not want to give it to me."

These are real, honest-to-goodness salespeople talking! Can you believe it?

If you have to make rough guesses at the amount of time it will take you to pull a quote together or coordinate with one of your team members, then guess! What's the worst that could happen? You call up the prospect's office to reschedule. Big deal.

Your objective

You didn't set the initial appointment for your health. You did it because you had an objective: helping to solve the prospect's problem with your product or service. You still have that objective at the conclusion of your initial visit. Therefore, it is altogether appropriate for you to ask to move the process along to the next stage before the meeting adjourns.

Unless you receive a firm, unequivocal "no" at the first meeting, there will always be a next stage to talk about. And the best possible time to set the appointment for discussing that next stage is right then. You both have your calendars within reach. You both have pens or pencils handy. What other time would you choose to set your next meeting? What on earth would induce you to leave that room without knowing when you will next meet with the person?

"Okay, Mr. Jones; I think we've gone about as far with this as we can today. What I'd like to do is meet with you a couple of weeks from now to show you exactly what we can do for your company. How's Friday the fifteenth?"

Listen for the response. (There has to be a response of some kind!) Then work from there with the information you receive.

Take Notes

Taking notes during your meeting with the prospect can be one of your most powerful sales tools. Taking notes will reinforce, both for you and the prospect, the reason you showed up in the first place: to learn more about the prospect's problem.

Listen
Taking notes helps you listen. There's something about having a blank sheet of paper in front of you that really tunes you in to what is being said and makes it more difficult to miss important points.

Show authority
Taking notes puts you in a position of authority and control. During the opening twenty minutes of most first-time sales visits, you can use all the help you can get.

Strengthen your analytical abilities
If you write down the highlights of your interview as it happens, you're using three senses: touch (your hand, which is doing the writing), hearing (what you have to do to listen

to the prospect), and sight (to see what you've written). My experience has been that by approaching a problem through tactile, visual, and aural stimuli, you're usually in a much better position to come up with a solution.

Get the prospect to share information

Taking notes will encourage the prospect to open up. Every time I conduct a seminar, I get further proof of how effective the simple act of writing something down (in this case, on an easel) can be in encouraging communication. When I simply stand in front of an audience and ask, "What was good about the presentation we just heard?" nothing happens. When I stand in front of an easel and write, "GOOD POINTS IN PRESENTATION" across the top, then ask for suggestions—wham! The room comes alive!

Position signals

Taking notes sends strong positive signals to the prospect. When the prospect says, "I have 500 trucks, each of which holds 75 widgets, making deliveries 320 days a year," sees that you've written "500 × 75 widgets × 320 days/yr," guess what? You've scored! You care! You're listening!

Some suggestions

I'd suggest you use a standard yellow pad with a hard cardboard backing, stiff enough for you to be able to write on while it's on your lap. Keep your notes clean and spare; they should be legible to both you and the prospect at all times. Where appropriate, draw oversized diagrams in your notes—and show your diagrams to the prospect.

Create a Plan with Each New Prospect

I go through a little monologue each time I meet a new prospect. I say, "Here's someone new. Here's someone I've never met before. What am I going to do that will be a little different with this person?"

It may be routine for you, but the prospect you're dealing with has never gone through the sales cycle with you before. One of the best ways to combat that "here I go again" sensation is to produce a customized, written plan for your prospect. This should be based on the material you gather in your notes during the first and subsequent meetings. After a while, you become familiar with certain objections or problems. And it's all too easy to pigeonhole your prospect. "I know that one; that's just like the problem the guy at ABC Company had." Well, it is and it isn't. It is not like the ABC problem in that the person who just outlined it has nothing to do with ABC Company, and he probably faces a number of different challenges.

A prospect who offers an objection is really making a gesture of good faith. By taking the time to share a concern or problem, your prospect is passing along important information on the way your product or service needs to be adapted. Listening is the first part of the secret, and identifying the mutually accepted solutions is the second.

Find out what those challenges are, and discover the unique circumstances or background your prospect may face. Then commit the solutions to paper, working with your prospect to determine the outline of the plan that will make the most sense in the current situation.

Doctor, doctor . . .

If you go to the doctor because you have a stomachache, you don't care if he's seen thousands of other people with stomachaches. The last thing you want is for him to rush in the room, look you up and down, mumble some technical phrase, and scratch something on a prescription pad before hustling away again.

No. You want him to ask how you feel, how long you've felt that way, whether you've ever felt that way before, exactly where it hurts, and any other pertinent questions. If a doctor does all that, you're likely to be a better patient—and you'll probably have a better attitude about coming to see him next time.

As a salesperson, you're a doctor. It doesn't matter how many patients you've seen before. This one is the only one you're seeing now. Include the patient in your diagnosis and treatment. Doing so not only makes for a better working atmosphere, it also increases the likelihood that your patient will have the positive attitude that is really the driving force behind so many dramatic recoveries!

Ask for Referrals

My favorite story about referrals has to do with a very successful salesperson I know named Bill. Every year he vacations in some exotic locale like Fiji or the Cayman Islands or Hawaii. Often, these vacations come as a result of company bonuses for his performance or industry awards. So about once a year, Bill sends a letter to his customers and qualified prospects announcing his return from paradise, where he received the XYZ Award for Outstanding Salesmanship. Bill's purpose in writing the letter is to thank his clients for their business and to make it perfectly clear that the only way he has been able to attain his goals is by helping customers attain theirs. Classy, yes?

At the end of the letter is a paragraph that runs something like this: "As you know, my business depends upon referrals. I would very much appreciate it if you would take a moment now to jot down the names and phone numbers of three or four people in the industry you feel might benefit from talking to me. Of course, if you do not wish me to use your name when contacting these people, all you have to do is indicate this in the space I've provided below. Again, thank you for your business, and here's to continuing success for both of us." Call me crazy. But I have a feeling there may be some cause-and-effect connection between letters like that and all those expensive vacations and impressive sales awards.

The numbers speak

Let's play a little multiplication game. Suppose five people give you five referrals each, for a total of twenty-five. Of those new referrals, suppose that 60 percent turn around and give you five referrals, too. That's fifteen times five, or seventy-five new prospects. Now, of those seventy-five, let's say another 60 percent gives you five referrals each . . . you get the picture. If you're out to build your client base exponentially (and why wouldn't you?), you'll have trouble finding a better place to start than asking for referrals.

Referrals are the lifeblood of a successful career in sales. And yet salespeople are usually terrified to ask for them.

Often, they feel it will somehow threaten the relationship they've built up with a customer to ask about other associates who might benefit from their product or service. Perhaps the customer really doesn't like using the product or service after all, and asking for a referral will only intensify that feeling or bring it to the surface.

Conservatism is one thing. Paranoia is another.

Follow your instincts

You should be able to tell without too much difficulty whether or not you have a satisfied customer or an enthusiastic prospect. If you do, what that really means is that you have established the foundations of a productive, mutually beneficial relationship. Why on earth wouldn't your customer want to share that kind of relationship with his friends and associates? Assuming there is no competitive or other business conflict involved, there is every reason in the world to expect a referral—and one passed along happily and enthusiastically!

How can you make referrals work for you? Let's say your goal is to get five new prospects for the week. Carry with you at all times a package of three-by-five index cards. After you're done meeting with one of your customers or a good-quality prospect, simply say something like this.

"Mr. Jones, I'm willing to bet there are people in your (industry, area, related businesses) who could benefit from my talking to them about this (product/service)."

As you say this, you take out five index cards. Hold them in your hand. Let the prospect or customer see that there are five of them there. Then say, "Do you know five people I could talk to?"

Help your contact along. It will be easier than you think; the fact that there are five separate index cards will make the task comprehensible and immediate. Your confident, professional attitude will guarantee that your request will not be seen as inappropriate.

Put the cards in a row on the desk as you fill them out, writing names only. Then, after you have identified the five referrals by name, go back and ask for the company affiliations, addresses, or other contact information. You do this because you want to make the first and most important job, identifying the people you can talk to, as easy as possible.

The direct approach

I know of one salesperson who will actually ask his contact at this point, "Frank, how would you feel about calling these people for me?" Of course, the contact says no and says the salesperson should make the call. Then the salesperson says, "Yeah, you're right, I probably should call them. You don't mind if I use your name, I hope?" He has never yet been turned down on the second question, which was the one he wanted a "yes" answer to in the first place.

That's an aggressive approach, and it's not one I'm sure I'd recommend to all salespeople. But it certainly illustrates the point that you can profit enormously when it comes to referrals by taking the initiative and asking for what you want!

HABIT #16

Show Enthusiasm

No, this doesn't mean embracing your prospect, pumping hands twenty times as you shake, or issuing endless implausible compliments about dress or appearance.

There is a difference between enthusiasm and poorly disguised panic. Enthusiasm builds bridges. Panic tears them down.

A sales meeting is like any other interaction. It takes a certain amount of time to get off the ground. If you understand the dynamics at work when you first come into contact with a prospect, you will go a long way toward understanding how enthusiasm must be conveyed as the relationship progresses.

The early phase

When people meet someone new, they pass through a number of stages. There is among human beings a certain feeling-out process, an introductory stage. At this stage, because the two of you don't know each other well enough yet, you cannot convincingly say all that you might want to about solving the prospect's problem. The prospect—along with most of the rest of the adult members of our species—requires a certain "choosing" time before entering into a socialization stage with another person. So the best way to show enthusiasm in the very early part of the meeting is to underplay it. Confident bearing; good eye contact (but not to such a degree it could be confused with staring); a firm handshake; predictable, smooth movements as you walk from one point to another—these are the keys to communicating your excitement about the new relationship you're trying to build.

The later phase

Only you can tell when the prospect enters the second stage of socialization, but rest assured that the change will be noticeable. It will be marked by a more relaxed, open approach, often reflected in less constricted body language. What you're looking for is the point at which the prospect listens not because he has agreed to do so, but because he wants to. Once you see that shift take place—and it may be during the first visit or during a subsequent one—you can change the "grammar" of your presentation.

You may decide to use your hands more in gesturing, or to use the prospect's preferred form of address ("Mr. Powers" or "Bill") somewhat more frequently. You might even feel comfortable using less formal phrasings and word choices: "Take a look for yourself." "How about that?" "And I'll tell you what we did."

Make an effort to avoid repetitive, mechanical gestures or responses. This is exactly what constitutes a less-than-spontaneous, unenthusiastic meeting. If your conversational partner insisted on constantly nodding his head up and down, with little real regard for what you had to say, how would you feel?

Keep your eyes open

These are general guidelines; your individual interactions with prospects will vary because prospects themselves will vary. The point is that bolstering your presentation with appropriate enthusiasm (especially on the second and subsequent visits) is an essential part of good salesmanship.

Habit #17

Give Yourself Appropriate Credit

Talk about yourself—but be humble

The two instructions are not mutually exclusive. You must learn how to do both. There's nothing wrong with walking into the prospect's office and talking with confidence and pride about what you do. Too many salespeople don't seem to grasp that that's really the reason they show up in the first place! The only trap to watch out for is that of appearing arrogant. Fortunately, that's easy enough to avoid.

A balanced confidence

When you walk in to meet the prospect, you will want to convey success, confidence, and flexibility. That's not arrogance. That's professionalism, and you should be proud of it. You should be able to talk, in detail, about the things that make you successful.

I don't suggest you play one-up with your prospect by boasting about how great your kids look, how good your golf game is, or how much money you make. That's a game you can't win, no matter how the conversation ends.

At the same time, I do believe aggressive promotion of your ability to succeed at your chosen job is a good idea—but one that requires a good deal of discretion on your part. You have to learn how to read the situation. You have to know when to step back. You have to know that what works for Prospect A in one situation may not work at all with Prospect B in another.

There is the very real risk that, if you don't read the signals correctly, you may overwhelm your prospect. But it's still worth thinking about, because far too many salespeople underwhelm the prospect, and that's just as dangerous. At least with my way, you know there's no way you're going to fade into the anonymous parade of mediocre salespeople most decision-makers have to face!

Talk yourself up

Yes. There is a definite risk. But in my view, it's a risk worth taking.

Try it with the next prospect you see.

"Mr. Jones, I am really glad to see you. This has been a really big week for us—we just completed the XYZ project. Let me tell you about it."

Wow! Here's a person who makes things happen!

In an earlier chapter, we used a doctor/patient analogy. I'm going to revise it a little bit to make a different point here.

This time, suppose you walk into the doctor's office—and the minute the doctor walks in the door, you notice that he looks sicker than you do. He's wheezing and coughing—and holding a stubby, half-smoked cigarette between his fingers. He's tottering a little bit as he walks. His eyes are yellowish. He's having trouble focusing on things.

Is this the man who's going to solve your health problem?

For many professionals, there are two kinds of people: those who add value to whatever they touch, and those who cause the value of everything they touch to decline. Prove that you fall into that first category. Show your value! Demonstrate it! Broadcast it! Shout it from the rooftops! As long as you do so without affecting an air of superiority, your self-promotion will be perceived as security. Not arrogance, but admirable, enthusiastic, security in your own mission and your ability to carry it out.

Tell the Truth
(It's Easier to Remember)

Someone did a university study recently on the issue of exactly how many white lies the average person tells during the course of a day. (Don't ask me how or why someone takes it into his head to study such a thing, or how he convinces someone else to pay for it.) Can you guess the results?

The answer came out to be approximately 200.

That's a lot of lying! And that's only the average. But let's be clear about what the researchers were looking for. When they went out looking for white lies, they were looking for all the times someone said to someone else, "I'm glad you could come by today," when in fact maybe the person wasn't so glad. Those kinds of falsehoods—which we could also classify as harmless social convention—aren't what I'm warning against when I advise you to tell the truth to your client.

Building bridges

Salespeople are relationship oriented. They build relationships on trust and personal contact, and they live and die on the strength of those relationships. That this is the case serves as a convincing argument for telling the occasional white social lie—and against telling any other kind of lie. Let's look at a couple of examples.

"Gee, this is really a great office. I sure wish I worked in a place like this." (Actually, the office you work in easily outshines the prospect's.)

No big deal. Some salespeople find it easier to make contact with the prospect by finding something like this to mention as they break the ice. What's the problem if there's a slight exaggeration on a point like this? Even if the prospect should somehow learn the terrible truth that you work in a spectacular office, is there any real downside to such a statement made tactfully, and without any overbearing flourishes? No.

"And about the delivery time you're asking for. I don't think we should have any problem meeting that, though I will have to clear it with the technical people after we square away the paperwork here today." (Actually, you know full well that you will miss the prospect's requested date by two weeks no matter what you say to the people in production.)

Red light! You are attempting to build a new relationship with a potential customer by deliberately misrepresenting your ability to solve his problem to his satisfaction. When things go awry later on—and nine times out of ten in this situation, they will—the prospect is not going to remember the cute little disclaimer you slid in there about running things by the technical people. He's going to remember that you said you could deliver the product on the first, and the blankety-blank thing didn't make it into the warehouse until the fifteenth. At that stage, you will no longer be regarded as a problem-solver. You will be regarded as a problem: a salesperson who promises more than can be delivered. This is not the stuff of which repeat sales are made.

The slippery slope

If you need further convincing, consider this. Once you make a habit of simply telling everyone what they want to hear, you're eventually going to run into a serious problem: You won't be able to keep your story straight. You'll be dealing with fifteen different clients, each of whom has received fifteen different, customized pie-in-the-sky assurances. It will only be a matter of time until you become hopelessly muddled . . . and slip up disastrously.

Don't risk it. Tell the truth; it's easier to remember.

Sell Yourself on Yourself

Following are some ideas you can use to motivate yourself. Use them!

Don't listen to the radio during your morning commute

Radio broadcasts are usually filled with lots of depressing news that you won't be able to do anything about anyway. You'll hear soon enough about any news of consequence; take the morning for yourself. Buy some motivational CDs or podcasts and make a habit of making the drive (or ride) in to work a time for positive messages and clear-headed, sober assessments of the day ahead. I know of one salesperson so committed to this principle that he honestly does not know whether his car radio even works!

Be specific with your goals—and your rewards

Perhaps your dream is to own a Lamborghini. Fine. Put a photo of one on your desk or on your refrigerator at home. Or perhaps you look at things a bit more analytically: Your goal is to close six new sales over the next month. Take a piece of paper and commit the goal in writing. This will make your aims more tangible and increase the likelihood that they will be attained.

Get positive reinforcement

I think it's fascinating how many successful sales "teams" there are—two individuals who sell completely independently, but who rely on each other for constant support, advice, and constructive criticism. For most of us, this really is a far better alternative than going it alone. If you can establish such a relationship in your current work environment, give it a try and see what happens.

Get outside

Yes, you do need a lunch break. No, you shouldn't work through the noon hour. (My studies on this with salespeople lead me to believe that those who make a point of putting work aside for an hour and getting outside in the sunshine are actually more productive in terms of sales volume than those eager beavers who don't know when to quit.)

Leave yourself notes

"I can do it." "Most of the things I worry about never happen." "I have solved the problems of over 500 customers." Try to leave one on your desk Friday afternoon; you'll probably forget about it until Monday morning, when it will be a pleasant surprise.

Keep things in perspective

At my office, we make a habit of issuing a humorous reminder to each other: "It's not brain surgery." It isn't! Missed calls, forgotten deadlines, problems with customers . . . challenging as they all can be, really aren't the end of the world. Sometimes things seem larger than they are. Try to keep that in mind as the day progresses. (For me, this lesson is particularly important between about two and four in the afternoon, when the day really can start to seem like an unending series of brain surgery projects. Is there a similar time for you? If so, that's when you should be sure to give yourself a break!)

HABIT #20

Start Early

Did you know that you can often get past the "secretary trap" by making your important cold calls before 9:00 a.m.?

A lot of decision makers are given to making it into the office before the rest of the crowd shows up. They might just pick up their own phone if you call them then. That's one obvious advantage to getting an early start on the day. There are also a number of others. For one thing, you'll be in a much better position to handle the office-wide crisis mentality that seems to set in around 9:01. For another, you'll be able to do your relaxing newspaper-shuffling and paperwork-managing at some time other than the peak contact hours during the business day. As I'm fond of pointing out, a salesperson is a lot like a retail store in that location is often the key requirement for success—only our location is the number of people you talk to during the day.

Commuting

There's more. My guess is that you'll find your commute a great deal easier if you get an earlier start in the morning.

That may seem like a minor consideration—until you realize how important attitude is in sales work. In so many of our big cities these days, you can spend an hour or an hour and a half simply getting from Point A to Point B in the morning. That's a lot of time, but the key consideration is really the aggravation you're likely to run into during that much drive time (or train or bus time, for that matter).

If you spend the first ninety minutes of every morning swearing at people or scowling at stoplights, you will probably find that your first few calls of the day are less than stellar. You'll lose the hop on your fastball before you talk to even a single potential customer—and that's a shame.

Making sure you're at your best

Finally, let me add an important observation, one based on my experiences and those of many of the successful salespeople I've worked with. The day really does seem to go better if you take a couple of moments of quiet time for yourself before charging into the fray. There's something very hard on the system about bursting through the door at 8:59 and having to hit the ground running, no matter what that entails.

I have a strong feeling that salespeople who do this cost themselves sales. The first few calls they make in the morning are warm-ups, whether they like it or not. (Of course, the best of all possible worlds would be to show up for work early enough to have a little time for oneself, and then do some role-playing with a colleague to make sure the warm-up calls aren't directed at live prospects.)

HABIT #21

Read Industry Publications
(Yours and Your Clients')

Quick! What kind of people do you suppose read *American Highway Engineer?*

How about *Publishers Weekly*? What audience do you expect would subscribe to *Adweek*? Or to *Billboard*?

You may not find them on a lot of newsstands, but these publications, and hundreds more like them, may be the most important magazines you can get your hands on. The industry or industries you work in almost certainly have some sort of trade journal or magazine read by just about anyone of any consequence within the field. You can put yourself at a distinct competitive advantage in comparison with many salespeople by becoming familiar with these publications. Use them to keep abreast of industry trends. You should understand and be able to adapt to the business environment faced by your customers.

Subscriptions tend to be expensive, but you can probably find back issues of the magazine or journal you're looking for in any good big-city library. Additionally, many publications offer their content online for free.

Your winning edge: information

You will probably find that you can get much better understanding of the technical jargon employed in your target group by reading the articles in trade and professional magazines. Of course, you may have some trouble with a few of the denser articles aimed at subgroups within an industry, but you're much better off puzzling things through on paper now than nodding your head vacantly when the terms are rattled off later!

The "who's who" or "on the move" sections of these publications can be a particularly fertile source of sales leads. In these columns, you will find the names and company affiliations of people who have recently been promoted or hired at a given company. Who wouldn't be flattered by a brief note of congratulations on having appeared in such a column—followed up by a phone call a few days later to talk about your company's product or service?

Keeping track of it all

You might even decide to keep a running clip file on references to the various companies or individuals appearing in trade magazines. This can be an invaluable aid in breaking the ice when meeting with a new prospect. For my part, I can tell you right now that I'd much prefer being able to cite three interesting points about a prospect culled from the pages of a trade magazine than be forced to talk for twenty minutes about the weather or how attractive the prospect's kids are!

HABIT #22

Support Your Visit the Next Day

Call or write your prospect the day after your visit. The vast majority of salespeople mean to do this but never get around to it. Build these contacts into your daily schedule or tickler system so you can be absolutely certain to follow up during that crucial period after the meeting.

Don't try to initiate contact any later than one day after the visit with the prospect. The whole point of this "supporting" maneuver is to re-establish your presence and your commitment to solving the prospect's problems.

What it might sound like in a telephone call

"Mr. Smith, this is Maude Powers at InfoWorld, Inc. I wanted to take a minute to thank you for taking time out of your schedule to meet with me yesterday. You know, I thought that meeting went really well. What did you think?"

I mention the phone contact first because it seems to be the most likely means of communication for such a message in today's sales environment. But an old-fashioned typed or printed letter on company stationery can win a good deal of positive attention. It's less likely to happen, of course, because time is at such a premium these days (and because so many salespeople honestly don't care to write letters). But that can work to your favor: your courteous, neat, well-written letter will stand alone.

Hard copy is more effective than e-mail, which has come to be thought of as something you dash off quickly when you're in a rush. A letter, though, implies thought.

Don't rattle on and on in this piece of correspondence. The letter you send should be very brief!

Take a look at the following model. Your letter should resemble it fairly closely.

Sept. 24, 2008

Dear Mr. Smith:

I wanted to drop a line to thank you for taking time out of your busy schedule to meet with me yesterday.

I found the ideas we exchanged very exciting, and I think you'll agree that there is the potential for a mutually beneficial relationship between your firm and ours. Mr. Smith, I hope you will feel free to call me if there are any questions or problems I can help you resolve.

Sincerely,
(written signature)
Maude Powers
(508) 555-1212

Give Speeches to Business and Civic Groups

Public speaking rates high on humanity's list of common fears. Yet I'm going to suggest that you take the time to develop your skills as a speaker and get out and share your (unparalleled!) expertise in your field with audiences—and not just audiences of people in your industry. Just about any audience, believe it or not, will do the trick.

The expert speaks

There is a double-edged sword at work here. First off, you will benefit tremendously from the boost in confidence you receive from being treated as an expert in your field. By the way, if you don't consider yourself an expert in your field, you shouldn't be selling in it. Your customers are certainly counting on your expertise!

Think about it. You know your subject. You talk about it all day long. Once you can make the minor adjustment of being able to give a lecture about what you do, you'll be a lecturer. Get someone to note you, and you'll be a "noted lecturer." Pretty soon, there may well be a lot of people noting you. Then you'll be a "widely noted lecturer." And deservedly so!

So the first benefit is reinforcement. You may know intellectually that you and your firm possess everything necessary to solve problems A, B, and C, but, believe me, you will receive an extraordinary emotional charge from actually getting up on stage and talking about A, B, and C to a group of willing listeners. If you don't think that that affirmation will carry over positively into the way you deal with prospects, my guess is you haven't been in sales very long.

The second benefit is even more remarkable. Studies have shown that when salespeople and consultants give speeches, on average, about one in ten audience members will seek out the speaker afterwards to ask about his or her services. What this really means is that 10 percent of any given audience you talk to will end up qualifying itself— and entering your prospect cycle! Who knows what might happen if you actually took the initiative to shake some hands and pass out business cards during intermissions and at the event's conclusion?

It may take some effort on your part to get to the point where you feel comfortable addressing a group, but I assure you the effort will be worth it. Remember that even the most accomplished professional speakers complain of stage fright. Your goal should not be to get every butterfly out of your stomach but to learn to make the adrenaline work for you.

Where to go to give the speech? Well, outside of the channels that may exist in your industry (such as addressing a trade conference or taking part in an annual convention), consider contacting your chamber of commerce about local round tables. Other possibilities include your area's Rotary Club, Kiwanis Club, or any group that seems relevant to the economy of your community or tied in somehow to what you do.

Go for it!

Go to the club or organization you've targeted, state your case, and see what happens. More often than not, they'll be glad to work you into the schedule.

So ask yourself, "What have I got to lose?" Absolutely nothing! If it doesn't work out, at least you've made an effort—and gotten your name out in front of that many potential prospects. Give public speaking a try. Believe me, more than one salesperson has benefited tremendously from taking this route!

Habit #24

Pass Along Opportunity When Appropriate

"What goes around, comes around."

This is a hard adage for a lot of salespeople to relate to, but it is nevertheless a vitally important point.

Lending a hand

Maintaining a can-do attitude where your own efforts are concerned is easy enough. But why on earth should you make an effort to help someone else out if you don't have to—if there seems to be no logical way for that person to help you out somewhere down the line in your career?

The answer is complicated. Perhaps the best illustration I can give is to offer an example from the world of baseball.

Have you ever noticed that, after a baseball player hits a single, he will often joke around a little bit with the first baseman on the opposing team? That's a little odd, isn't it? Considering that these are top-echelon professional competitors dealing with members of the opposition, you'd expect a sterner, uncompromising mindset. But there they are joking, nodding, smiling at one another.

You usually don't hear what they're saying. Interestingly enough, it turns out that, both on the basepaths and in their other contacts, opposing players often discuss some aspect of the game they play for a living. Of course, they're not giving away important strategy points that would give any competitive advantage in the game at hand. But they are often discussing points of interest that concern their own development as ballplayers. Even though they may be on opposite teams, two shortstops, for instance, will often discuss the irregularities of the surface in a given park, or pass along information on how to play a member of a third team in another city who has managed to scoot a few too many hits through the infield lately.

They pass along these facts not because they do not see each other as competitors (they do!), but because they also see each other as colleagues—and it's not a bad idea to be known as the type of person who likes to help out a colleague. You might get your own hot tip on how to play that new guy who's tearing up the league! You don't know you're going to get such a tip, but because you're "part of the grapevine," you'll certainly get whatever is circulating.

Let me note here before I'm inundated with mail from baseball fans about this that I'm talking about general trends among most ballplayers. You do find the occasional hard-nosed type who refuses to share a kind word with an opposing player, but that's the exception, not the rule. Many of these tight-lipped players are rookies whose main focus is on learning the ropes and remaining in the major leagues and not on contributing to "the book"—which is what baseball players call the collection of accepted, widely circulated strategies currently influencing decisions among all teams.

Adding to "the book"

Is there a "book" in your league? If so, do you contribute to it? Do you share insights, leads, and contacts with others where appropriate, even though you cannot see any immediate benefit in doing so? There are hundreds, probably thousands of stories about strange, off-the-wall referrals that were generated through the grapevine and that resulted in sales. To get your share, you'll need to develop a reputation as a person who contributes to that common pool of resources, tips, and openings.

Pass along opportunity when you can. It's a wise investment—one I've never heard any salesperson regret making.

Take Responsibility for Presentations that Go Haywire

Assuming personal responsibility for the sale is a remarkably effective sales tool. It works so well that, if you're like me, the first time you hear about the technique, you'll probably wonder why on earth you didn't incorporate it into your sales routine long ago.

To start with, you have to be utterly, completely convinced in your own heart that you can offer your prospect the best possible solution to his problem. If that confidence isn't there, the technique I'm about to describe simply won't work. If the prospect (or anyone else) asks you to talk about your firm, you have to be able to reply with sincerity that you work for a one-of-a-kind, customer-first company and are proud to do so.

When you're on a sales visit, and you come to the closing stage, you simply ask the prospect when the best time would be for the product to be delivered or the service to start. One of two things will happen. Either the prospect will answer your question receptively—and thereby become a customer—or the prospect will back off and say no. If you find yourself facing the second scenario, you take responsibility.

Surprise!

At this point, the salespeople I know who use this technique are genuinely taken aback—even shocked. And it's not an act. They believe in their company so completely, and know so much about the prospect by this stage of the game, that they are legitimately concerned to see any evidence of a negative response to the proposal they've made. And they state that concern in no uncertain terms. You can, too.

Here's what you say: "Mr. Jones, I'm really not sure what to say. I am so convinced that we have the best service, the best pricing, the best customization, and the best reputation of any firm in our industry that I can think of only one reason for you not to sign on with us. And that's that I must have done something terribly wrong just now in giving my presentation. So I'm going to ask you to give me a hand, Mr. Jones, and tell me where I went off course. Because, to be quite frank with you, sir, I know this service is right for you, and I'd really hate to have made a mistake like that."

What do you think you'll hear in response? One thing's for sure. It's not going to be easy for the prospect to come back with a run-of-the-mill brush-off like, "It's just not up our alley, Maureen." No, if you're Mr. Jones, you probably respect the person who had the courage to say that to you, who believes so strongly in the service you're looking at.

You're going to pass along information—information on exactly what the problem is with your firm's signing on.

The common response you'll hear after you take responsibility for the initial "no" will sound something like this: "No, no, no, Maureen, it has nothing to do with you. It's on our end." And the prospect can then be expected to go into detail about the remaining obstacles. Then you have the facts you need to continue through the cycle.

Be sure you can deliver!

Let me repeat: This can be a startlingly effective technique, but it requires absolute faith on your part that you can in fact deliver on your promises. There is another catch, as well: You have to be willing to put aside the common fixation with being right that we all share to a degree.

But when it comes right down to it, would you rather be right—or close a sale?

No One Wakes Up and Says, "I'm Going to Be Stupid Today"

People make mistakes. You've had it happen to you. You check and double-check what you're about to do and then, Bam! Something goes wrong.

It's easy to be understanding about mistakes—when someone else makes them. But when *you* make an error, it somehow seems worse. Because the process is so intense, because there is so much riding on the outcome, mistakes in the sales process seem magnified—at least in the eyes of the salesperson.

I've seen this too often not to know that it's true. Salespeople place such a great emphasis on being right that they excessively and needlessly criticize themselves for even the simplest of mistakes. Inevitably, that ends up affecting their work.

I had a guy working for me who exhibited this pattern one time because he'd lost a couple of deals he absolutely, positively thought were going to happen. However, he did a couple of stupid things that just threw him off his game. He made a mistake on a sales call. It was a stupid mistake, misreading a client's personality. Then he misspelled another client's name. Because he knew it was stupid, he went into a funk. That funk led to a slump from which he was unable to recover.

The slump was serious, almost a depression.

No matter how hard he tried, for the longest time he could not get an appointment. If you've been in sales for any length of time, you've probably had this happen to you or to someone you know.

Just as in baseball, once you get in a slump, it's hard to get out of it. The problem is that when it happens to a ball player, he still cashes his million-dollar checks. When it happens to you, commission checks disappear.

What to do? Some people say take a vacation—get away for a week or so and come back refreshed. Do it if you want to, but that's not from the Steve Schiffman School of Antidotes. You're not making sales. Boo-hoo. Work your way out of it.

Remember, attitude is money (a saying so powerful that I remember it with the acronym AIM). When you're in a funk, people sense it, and they will play into your negativity. Instead, concentrate on something you do well. If it's prospecting, spend an inordinate amount of time doing that. If it's presentations, spend extra time on the next few you have scheduled. If all else fails, do a no-brainer, and work on a simple account you can sell blindfolded with your hands tied behind your back. Do anything that will restore your confidence and turn that negative attitude into a positive one. Suddenly you'll find yourself back on a roll.

Whatever you do to set your ship right, do it immediately. Nip your funk in the bud by dealing with the problem right away. Don't wait for a downward spiral to begin. If you make a mistake, no matter how stupid it is, remember that it's just a mistake. Move on. Apologize to the client and get over yourself. Don't for one minute think that the prospect hasn't made a mistake or done something much worse. Everyone knows you didn't wake up that morning and tell yourself, "Gee, today I think I'll be stupid." Stuff happens. Move on.

The bottom line, again, is that mistakes happen. That's why they're also called *errors*. In fact, sometimes, even when you do the right thing, matters end badly. One of my favorite books is *The Logic of Failure,* by Dietrich Dörner. It's about how to avoid failures and one of the examples he uses has stayed with me.

A small town was in a tourist area that didn't get much business from people driving from Tourist Site A to Tourist Site B. So the town fathers decided to put speed bumps down the main street to slow traffic down and allow travelers to get at least a quick glimpse at the merchandise in store windows. And it worked.

Drivers slowed down, stopped, parked their cars, and shopped on Main Street. Merchants were ecstatic . . . for a while. Then they started hearing complaints from their regular customers.

Little by little, the locals started to avoid the town, and eventually the town council removed the bumps and put the town back in the same position it was in before. Here's a town board that made absolutely the right mistake, which turned into the wrong mistake, one that ultimately had severe consequences for the town. No one on the board woke up on the day of the vote and said, "You know, today I'm going to be stupid." They gave it a lot of thought and did what they thought was right. Get over it.

Finally, there are times when it's okay—even beneficial—to be wrong. You're meeting with a prospect or have mined deeply into the Power of Twelve. You come back to your contact and say "Look, this is what I've come up with, and here is what I base it on."

Your customer can agree, but it is just as good if he finds errors in your analysis. By correcting you, he becomes part of your process. When you use the information he provides, you enlist him in your effort. On at least a subconscious level, he becomes a supporter of yours, an ally. How can he vote against you when you use his information? The sales process is one in which it is important for you to be "righted."

This part of the process in which you verify what you've learned is crucial to the sale and allows you to be wrong. And this, in turn, allows the potential customer to not only correct you but give you his perception of what is needed.

The Customer Isn't Always Right

That the customer is always right is one of the Ten Commandments of Sales. It is a law that has been passed down from generation to generation: Don't ever tell customers they're wrong; you don't want to rile them up.

So what I'm about to suggest is blasphemous.

It ain't necessarily so.

I believe that good salesmanship (or saleswomanship, for that matter) is a partnership between the salesperson and his customer. The salesperson can't make significant progress without the cooperation of his clients and, frankly, that's true the other way around as well. For that to work, you have to trust each other and be able to communicate honestly.

I know it's not easy. The salesperson has to have strength of purpose, confidence in his abilities, and the knowledge that he brings something to the table. You're not just a salesperson; you're a consultant with unique expertise.

Where do you get the right to say that the customer is wrong? Who knows more about what you're selling than you do? Who spends more time thinking about the product, the way it works and how to sell it? No one.

Here's a quick example of what I mean. I was brought in by a theme park company to discuss holding training sessions for its sales force. As always, I did my Power of Twelve to examine what the company was doing and what I could bring to the table.

More often than not, I'll find some element of the sales process that needs improvement. Then I'll suggest a course on, say, presentation skills or prospecting. But what I found was something completely different. To my mind, the company's sales strategy was wrong. I could have gone in and pitched a sales course the way I always do. That would have been the safe route. I'm confident that by merely improving their skills, the company's numbers would improve—even though the salespeople were selling a faulty strategy. I could have taken my money and walked away.

But I really do believe in what I write. I am sincere when I say good sales is a partnership. The theme park company sold corporate picnics—but not many. The picnics didn't have any real structure. The salespeople could never explain what the picnics were about.

So I went back to my contact and told him the company was taking the wrong approach. He shouldn't be selling picnics; he should sell motivational get-togethers, opportunities to build camaraderie.

At first, the theme park folks weren't comfortable with what I said, but to their credit allowed me to come in and give it a try. The result was that by the end of the first year, sales had increased by 25 percent. Buoyed by that early success (created by the sales force), the company revamped its collateral material. Soon, it was not only selling more "picnics" than ever before, but the events were larger than they'd previously managed to attract.

To me this is a perfect example of a salesperson telling a customer he's wrong.

Of course, tact is always helpful. You can say you disagree with what a customer does or says, but you also must be able to say "Here's why" or "I have another idea." Simply put, you need to be able to explain your thinking.

The best way to get your feelings across is to say, "I have an idea" or "Imagine." *Imagine* is a powerful word in the sales vocabulary. When I say, "Imagine the Eiffel Tower," that's all you think about. When I say, "Imagine your people making more appointments using this system instead of your current one," customers can see the picture and seize the moment.

Too many salespeople are afraid to make these kinds of statements, in part, I believe, because they don't have proper product knowledge. They don't know their product's malleability, or how it can be changed and adapted to meet a particular customer's needs. That's the knowledge you need to have the confidence to become a true partner.

Be Honest with Yourself about the Nature of the Firm You Work For

In my speeches and seminars, I often equate business with war, noting that each field of endeavor demands sound planning, has winners and losers, requires ammunition, features a chain of command, and so on. And I always conclude my remarks in this area by pointing out that business does have a few major advantages over war. Nobody gets killed, and you can change armies.

Look at your job and yourself

Changing armies and the honest self-assessment that is often required to do so are the issues at hand. If you're currently in a work environment that does not meet your personal standards for quality, ethics, or orientation toward the customer, you should consider moving on. Too often, salespeople will stay with an army that's all wrong for them. The reasons given can be endless—don't have time, don't have the contacts, it's not really that bad here, lack of visibility in the industry—but, in the final analysis, the reasons are all rationalizations, and unconvincing ones at that.

There is a danger here because sometimes salespeople, who are a persuasive lot, will often go to great lengths to sell themselves on an idea. If that idea doesn't really work, the possibility of denial and self-deception looms. You may have to be on your guard and make a special effort to be brutally honest with yourself about the direction both you and your firm are headed in.

Why? Because it's your career on the line. You want to work toward developing productive, mutually beneficial relationships with all the people you encounter on a professional level. If you find that your sales work now is not doing that for you—if you find that, to the contrary, you are leaving a trail of angry former customers in your wake—you are asking for trouble.

Games

Some salespeople try to play games with themselves. They try to rationalize a situation that is inherently manipulative or abusive and see it as something it isn't and will never be. Don't be one of them. Don't set yourself up for a fall.

You have to feel it in your gut; you have to believe in your cause. You have to know in the marrow of your bones that all of your efforts are in line with your value system and that that system encourages only productive, straight-shooter interactions. No matter how you identify your goals, you must be certain that it is right for you to pursue them. You must know instinctively the benefit people will derive from working with you, and you must believe in your heart that all your company's efforts are for the best.

Tell Everyone You Meet the Name of the Company You Work For and What You Sell

Why not?

Why not tell your doctor? Your electrician? Your dentist? The cab driver you rode with this morning? Your friend at another company? The person you sit next to on the airplane? Your barber? Members of the community group or charitable organization you work with? The guy sitting next to you at the ballgame?

Why not make a point of broadcasting your profession to anyone and everyone—with pride? I'm not suggesting you subject everyone you know to a sales pitch, of course. What I am suggesting is that it become second nature for you to say, loud and clear, to every single person you meet, bar none, that you're a salesperson for XYZ Corporation, maker of the finest widgets west of the Pecos. Couple that with a handshake and a confident, look-you-in-the-eye smile, and you know what? Every once in a while, someone's going to say, "Widgets, huh? You know, we've been thinking about those. . . ."

The secret

Far too many salespeople have a pathological aversion to letting people know what they do for a living. The only reason I can come up with for this is that we often aren't quite as proud of what we do for a living as a brain surgeon might be, or an attorney, or a teacher, or workers in any of dozens of categories who have no difficulty mentioning how they spend the majority of their waking hours.

We should be proud of being salespeople; I know I am! I know that the economy of the society I live in would not function without people who do what I do for a living, and I know that every transaction I undertake benefits all who are affected by it. Am I proud of that? You bet!

You should feel that way about your job, too. If you need to make some changes before you can feel that way, make the changes. Then look people in the eye and tell them what you do and who you do it for. Make it a habit. It may take a little work at first, but eventually you will begin passing along your name, profession, and company affiliation almost without thinking. (Here's a helpful hint: Current research indicates that a routine you stick with for twenty-one days will become ingrained as a permanent habit you incorporate automatically.)

If you have to, start small and work your way up. You might begin by choosing friends or contacts you know well enough to talk to but who don't yet know what you do for a living. But the easiest route by far is to say what you do for a living and who you do it for as you are intro-duced to someone. It's easier than you think, and it can pay tremendous dividends.

Keep Your Sense of Humor

Let's be honest. It can be tough to be a salesperson some-times. Paradoxically enough, that's exactly why sales work has to be funny now and then.

I can only pass along my own observations about the salespeople I've worked with: Laughing helps. And not just around the edges. Laughing helps a lot. Salespeople depend on a good self-image more than any other profes-sionals I know of, and it's awfully hard to keep a good self-image if you take yourself so seriously that you can't back off and laugh about the world once in a while.

Let me backtrack for a moment. One of the most scathing arguments against becoming a salesperson I know of is a very depressing film I saw some years back called *Salesman*. It's a documentary shot in grainy black-and-white about three traveling salespeople. It portrays sales as manipulative, demeaning, dishonest work—work that no thinking, feeling person would ever undertake voluntarily.

I have a real problem with that movie, for a couple of reasons. The first is that a great many people who aren't salespeople have been exposed to it, and they have formed unrealistic stereotypes about my profession as a result. The second is that most of us who are salespeople haven't been exposed to it, and haven't been able to see the debilitating results of consistently bad sales work. This movie is convincing proof of how dangerous a salesperson with the wrong attitude can be, both to customers and to the salesperson himself. If you're a salesperson—and especially a salesperson who takes his or her work very, very seriously—that movie will probably have a remarkable effect on you.

Mistakes

The salespeople in this film make just about every mistake in the book, including, but not limited to, failing to establish customer needs, lying to prospects, not listening to prospects, carrying a negative mental attitude, and failing to commit to their own ongoing professional development. But there's another error they make that, if it were rectified, could make all the other problems manageable.

They take the damned job too seriously and never give themselves a chance to decompress. It's difficult to attend to those other (admittedly catastrophic) problems if they've become part of your sales environment. But I can guarantee you here and now that there is no way on earth to approach your sales work the way it should be approached if you can't step back and laugh at yourself once in a while, preferably while on the job.

You matter!

You are too important a tool to yourself to run down. Take a break. Accept that it really is all right for you to miss the mark once in a while. Remember that you have to take the long view, and that today's catastrophe usually doesn't mean much tomorrow. This is a message that really never got to sink in as far as the salespeople in that movie were concerned. And they paid for it.

Don't let the world at large talk you into thinking you're not in charge of your day, your month, your career. After all, you're the one with the answers. You're the professional solver of problems. You're the one who stays in control by keeping your head, asking the right questions, and being precise when it comes to giving necessary advice.

Lighten up and win! And remember, success couldn't happen to a nicer person.

Quick Reference Summary

HABIT #1
If it doesn't work, fix it

There's no sense in perpetuating a bad habit just because you've always done it that way. Step away, re-examine your process, and figure out ways to shore up your weaknesses.

HABIT #2
Communicate the message that it is sound business to trust you

Don't cut corners at the expense of your own credibility—it's one of your most powerful weapons. Develop leadership skills. Build mutually beneficial long-term partnerships.

HABIT #3
Ask the right questions

Ease in with simple questions that get the prospect talking about himself, then move on to the past, the present, and the future—complementing each with why and how. Use middle-ground questions when appropriate, but beware of overreliance on them. You must take responsibility for keeping the cycle moving forward.

HABIT #4
Take the lead

Tell the prospect where you are at any given point in the sales cycle. Don't be afraid to steer the conversation in the direction you want it to go. If there are questions or problems, you'll hear about them—and that's what you want! When in doubt, take the initiative in a calm, professional manner.

HABIT #5
Listen, learn, and lead

The smarter you are, the better able you are to lead customers where you want them to go. Information is power, so dig deeply. Mine your prospects' knowledge, and use it to create sales.

HABIT #6
Engage the prospect

Don't play ping-pong—work from the unique set of verbal and non-verbal cues your prospect will supply. Discuss that with which you are comfortable and familiar. Discuss the surroundings. "Lean in" when the prospect begins to talk about himself. Show care by really caring.

HABIT #7
Find key requirements

"Find a need and fill it" has its limits. For most of us, the day of relying exclusively or primarily on first-time customers has passed. Find requirements you can fill among those sought-after, qualified buyers who know full well that the choice is theirs.

HABIT #8
Know the sales timetable

Do you know when to make a concerted pitch? Work backward from when your customer needs your product or service. Figure in the time it takes you to deliver. Then add on your usual sales time.

HABIT #9
Convert the leads that "fall into your lap"

The sale you deserve? Maybe. But take the time to establish a relationship and find out what's going on. Then ask to set up an in-person appointment. Don't assume you've got a sure thing!

HABIT #10
Know how to make your product or service fit somewhere else

Does what you sell work in only one way? Or can you make it serve some new function? Can you present it in a different light?

HABIT #11
Pretend you're a consultant (because you are)

Don't improvise. If you need to take time out to come up with a workable solution, do so. Solving problems is the name of the game—and you have to listen before you can come up with a solution.

HABIT #12
Ask for the next appointment while you're on the first visit

This is perhaps the simplest, easiest-to-follow piece of advice in this book. Don't make excuses—make appointments!

HABIT #13
Take notes

Taking notes during your meeting with the prospect helps you listen, puts you in a position of authority, encourages your prospect to open up, and sends positive signals.

HABIT #14
Create a plan with each new prospect

It may be routine to you, but the prospect has never gone through the sales cycle with you before. Produce a customized, written plan based on your notes from early meetings. Remember, you're the doctor—don't rush the diagnosis!

HABIT #15
Ask for referrals

Don't be shy—you can't afford it. Referrals are the lifeblood of a successful career in sales.

HABIT #16
Showing enthusiasm

Talk up your company—and remember that there is a difference between enthusiasm and poorly disguised panic. Enthusiasm builds bridges; panic tears them down.

HABIT #17
Give yourself appropriate credit

Talk about yourself—but be humble. (No, the two aren't mutually exclusive.) Convey success, confidence, and flexibility. Highlight past successes, but don't try to one-up the prospect. Try to exhibit the characteristics of a person who makes things happen.

HABIT #18
Tell the truth (it's easier to remember)
We tell, on average, 200 lies every day! Remember, your credibility is a precious asset. Defend it!

HABIT #19
Sell yourself on yourself
Motivate yourself! Avoid the radio during your morning commute; listen to motivational tapes instead. Be specific about your goals—and your rewards. Get positive reinforcement. Get outside. Leave yourself notes. Keep things in perspective.

HABIT #20
Start early
There is a world before 9:00 a.m.! You can beat the secretary trap, ease your commute, reduce your aggravation, and improve your attitude by making it in an hour or so before everyone else does.

HABIT #21
Read industry publications (yours and your clients')
Trade journals and newsletters (whether in print or online) are invaluable data sources; read them. These publications are fertile sources of leads, industry gossip, and important inside stuff.

HABIT #22
Support your visit the next day
Call or write your present prospect the day after your visit. The vast majority of people who mean to do this never actually get around to it. Build this step into your schedule!

HABIT #23
Give speeches to business and civic groups
You will benefit tremendously from the boost in confidence you receive from being treated as an expert in your field (which you are); in addition, an average of one in ten audience members will seek you out to ask about your services.

HABIT #24
Pass along opportunity when appropriate

"What goes around, comes around." Being a part of the grapevine is a wise decision, one I've never heard any salesperson regret making.

HABIT #25
Take responsibility for presentations that go haywire

Rejected? Try this: "Mr. Jones, I just don't understand . . . I must have made a mistake in my presentation for you to decide it this way. I know we can help you. Can you help me and show me where things went wrong?"

BONUS HABIT #1
No one wakes up and says, "I'm going to be stupid today"

Everyone makes mistakes. Get over it.

BONUS HABIT #2
The customer isn't always right

Forget the conventional wisdom. It's okay to tell a customer that there's a better way.

BONUS HABIT #3
Be honest with yourself about the nature of the firm you work for

If you have to choose between fighting a losing battle for losing generals and finding another army, find another army. Don't rationalize.

BONUS HABIT #4
Tell everyone you meet the name of the company you work for and what you sell

Why not make a point of broadcasting your profession to anyone and everyone—with pride? Simply pass along your name, profession, and company affiliation to every new person you meet.

BONUS HABIT #5
Keep your sense of humor

It can be tough to be a salesperson sometimes—but that's why sales work has to be funny now and then. Lighten up.

About the Author

Stephan Schiffman has trained over 500,000 salespeople at firms such as AT&T Information Systems, Chemical Bank, Manufacturers Hanover Trust, Motorola, and U.S. Healthcare. Mr. Schiffman, president of DEI Management Group, is the author of *Cold Calling Techniques (That Really Work!)*, *The 25 Most Common Sales Mistakes—and How to Avoid Them*, and a number of other popular books on sales.

Do you have questions, comments, or suggestions regarding this book? Please share them with me! Write to me at this address:

Stephan Schiffman
c/o Adams Media Corporation
57 Littlefield St.
Avon, MA 02322

Schiffman's *25 Sales Series*
Everything you need to beat your goals!

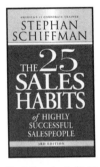

Trade Paperback, $6.95
ISBN 10: 1-59869-757-9
ISBN 13: 978-1-59869-757-5

Trade Paperback, $6.95
ISBN 10: 1-59337-014-8
ISBN 13: 978-1-59337-014-5

Trade Paperback, $6.95
ISBN 10: 1-55850-511-3
ISBN 13: 978-1-55850-511-7

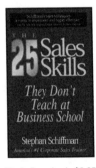

Trade Paperback, $6.95
ISBN 10: 1-58062-614-9
ISBN 13: 978-1-58062-614-9

Trade Paperback, $6.95
ISBN 10: 1-58062-116-3
ISBN 13: 978-1-58062-166-8